P9-DMQ-151

The Court of Two Sisters
COOKBOOK

The Court of Two Sisters

COOKBOOK

With a History of the French Quarter and the Restaurant by Mel Leavitt

PELICAN PUBLISHING COMPANY

Gretna 1992

For Joseph Fein, Jr.

Library of Congress Cataloging-in-Publication Data

Fein, Joseph.
    The Court of Two Sisters cookbook / Joseph Fein III, Jerome Fein,
Mel Leavitt.
      p. cm.
    ISBN 0-88289-866-3
    1. Court of Two Sisters (Restaurant)—History.
2. New Orleans (La.)—Buildings, structures, etc. 3. New Orleans
(La.)—History. 4. Cookery, American—
Louisiana style. I. Fein, Jerome. II. Leavitt, Mel., 1927- . III. Title.
TX945.5.C675F45 1991
641.5'09763'35—dc20   91-17110
                                                                  CIP

Manufactured in the United States of America

Published by Pelican Publishing Company, Inc.
1101 Monroe Street, Gretna, Louisiana 70053

Contents

Preface

"There are only three great storybook cities in America—" Tennessee Williams proclaimed, "New York City, San Francisco . . . and New Orleans."

The playwright left little doubt as to which one was his favorite. His masterpiece, *"A Streetcar Named Desire,"* was written in New Orleans' French Quarter, in a large garret room at the corner of St. Peter and Royal streets. Time and again he returned to this "19th-century city within a city" for inspiration; in fact, he kept an apartment in the Quarter for forty-two years.

From his skylight window he could look down Rue Royale, the fabled street of the old Creole aristocracy, of small shops and art galleries. Within a block was the epicenter of this timeless place, "Governor's Row." There, virtually *"dans le coeur du Vieux Carré"* (in the heart of the Old Square), stood the fabled Court of Two Sisters at 613 Royal Street.

This urban oasis, with its huge, evergreen courtyard, bubbling fountain, and sweet-scented foliage, dates back almost to the founding of New Orleans. The city's visionary "father," Bienville, laid out the first crude settlement in 1718. Fourteen years later (1732), French colonial records indicate that Bienville's successor, Etienne de Perier, second governor of Louisiana, resided in a mansion on this specific site.

There is also considerable evidence that Perier's successor, the flamboyant Grand Marquis de Vaudreuil, lived there too. It was the Grand Marquis who introduced the colony to its first *bal masque* (costumed Mardi Gras celebration) in the 1740s. He strove to create his own variation of Royalist France, a kind of petit Paris on the banks of the muddy Mississippi.

7

"Governor's Row" became the very pulse of early French Creole society. Five governors, two mayors, two state Supreme Court justices, and a future chief justice of the U.S. Supreme Court lived and/or worked at one time in the 600 block of Rue Royale. In fact, at one point an ambitious young attorney named Zachary Taylor, who was destined to become the 12th president of the United States, entered into the practice of law at 621 Royal Street.

Not far away, on Bourbon Street, Jean Lafitte, the pirate-patriot of a thousand tales, both real and imagined, ran a black-smith shop. Supposedly he and his brother, Pierre, forged iron-work by day and, nightly, plotted their various intrigues. A few blocks farther down, the shadowy sorceress Marie Laveau prac-ticed her peculiar brand of voodoo, peddling *gris-gris* bags and charms from her simple cottage on St. Ann Street.

Nouvelle Orleans was basically a French city for almost a hun-dred years. When the English-speaking Anglos arrived in force following the Louisiana Purchase in 1803, the proud Creoles (descendants of "those born in the colony") considered *"les Américains"* the foreigners. They felt that they were the true natives and they clung to their lifestyle and language long after the interlopers had gained dominance in political and eco-nomic affairs.

Following the Civil War and Reconstruction, the Creoles' fortunes waned. Among those affected were two Creole sisters, Bertha and Emma Camors. Widowed in their later years, they were virtually inseparable, and from all that history can tell us, indomitable as well. In 1886, they established at 613 Royal Street a *"rabais,"* or notion shop, which specialized in fancy gowns and dresses. They ran it for twenty years, until such time as their resources and their French-speaking clientele gave out.

They left the historic mansion on Governor's Row with a new and indelible name: The Court of Two Sisters. Today, this elegantly restored landmark encompasses a unique indoor-outdoor restaurant built around the largest patio in the Vieux Carré.

"The Court," as natives call it, continues to evoke memories of a unique culture inspired by the proud Creoles, who considered living an art in itself and cuisine the highest form of art. Creole cuisine is a distinctively New Orleans inspiration—a mixture of French, Spanish, Indian, and African cookery. The city's literature abounds with references to food and dining, its great Creole chefs and restaurants.

The Court of Two Sisters seems to have been destined to become a restaurant. Its exotic courtyard, lush with foliage, was the site of many a grand colonial *soirée*. The mansion, located in the bosom of Governor's Row, was a banquet place for visiting foreign dignitaries and the local elite more than 200 years ago.

Old New Orleans and the Court became synonymous with a way of life and an atmosphere unknown elsewhere in the United States. In a sense, both represent islands of detachment, if you will, from the often frantic hustle-bustle of today's high-speed, high-tech world.

You'll find a number of excellent, time-tested recipes within this volume, many of them unique to New Orleans and/or The Court of Two Sisters. Meanwhile, if there is a Creole recipe for living, I suppose it might read something like this: Do not rush. Do not hasten. Relax, *mon ami*, and enjoy this small haven. Here you can linger at your own pace and stroll through history leisurely, taking time to feel its "living presence." New Orleans, like its cuisine, is made to savor slowly, employing all of your senses. Once you've sampled it, you will not easily be satisfied with anything else.

Not a bad recipe to start with, *n'est-ce pas?*

Mel Leavitt

Part 1: The History

The French Quarter

Visitors have been trying to comprehend the peculiar romance and mystique of the original old city, the Vieux Carré (or French Quarter) for the better part of three centuries. It is another time, another place. Unmoved. Unmarred by 20th-century shrillness. The great cathedral's soft chime punctuates the evening stillness, and can startle one into realizing the reveries that the place engenders.

The first French settlers, a libertine bunch, arrived between 1718 and 1729, and were an unlikely sprinkling of aristocrats and smugglers, adventurers and speculators. *Nouvelle Orleans* was a small patch of slightly elevated ground a few feet above the level of the Mississippi that overlooked the broad "crescent" of the river as it swept, untrammeled, downward to the Gulf of Mexico.

It was an island city, surrounded on all sides by water and swamp. Some called it the *"Isle de Orleans."* Since most of it existed from four to six feet below sea level and was subject to frequent flooding, Parisians nicknamed it *"Le Flotant"*—The Floating Land.

French laws, French customs, and the French language were firmly established long before the first English-speaking "Kaintucks" came drifting downriver in their flatboats in 1780. Unable to battle the powerful river currents upstream (the first steamboat did not arrive until 1812), these crude American backwoodsmen sold their merchandise and then broke up the boats for bargewood and sold that for material to build cottages. (Others, ship captains from Europe, sold off their ballast [usually large stones] to homeowners wishing to pave their streets, sidewalks, and patios. Ballast stone was used to pave the porte-cochere (carriageway) at 613 Royal.)

13

The Americans, accustomed to blue laws, zoning laws, and solid ground, were astonished. The attitude toward life was celebrant— "Live and Let Live" was the motto. One New England matron exclaimed, "They celebrate Sundays the way we do the Fourth of July." The French Market and the entire city resembled a perpetual convention of nations and races, as wave upon wave of immigrants poured in. Lastly, the whole place threatened at each moment to sink into the wet soil. "These Frenchmen have built a city where God never intended a city to be built," said one.

The native Creoles were amused by their reactions. "It is better," they said, "to live life to the fullest, *sans* regret, than never to live at all." Then they added, "The greatest sin, *mes amis*, is boredom."

The original French city has remained aloof, timeless, detached, and generally undisturbed since two great fires ravaged it in 1788 and 1794. The original Vieux Carré became literally a city within a city; it is the oldest city plat, or permanent grid, in the United States that remains intact as it was originally surveyed and mapped. The close configuration, the streets, and the street names are the same as when the original Vieux Carré was laid out in 1722 by Adrien Pauger.

Today the French Quarter survives, not as a monument or a tourist attraction, but as a living, breathing, functioning 19th-century city—the "only intact 19th-century city in North America." It is protected as an ensemble by a stringent set of codes and laws, carefully preserved and buffered from unnecessary intrusions.

In certain ways, the French Quarter seems as much Spanish colonial as anything else (the Spanish ruled the city from 1766-1803). When the original buildings burned down, the Spanish administered the initial rebuilding. Most of the architects, however, were French Creole or American.

Regardless, the architectural style is strictly indigenous to New Orleans, and is a brilliant adaptation to the terrain and climate. Like so many inventions that distinguish this "island city"—Jazz,

Mardi Gras, Creole cooking—it draws its enduring grace from two centuries of Franco-Spanish experience in similar semi-tropic, rainy, humid climes. The roots, which are supremely adapted to this special place, lie as much in the Mediterranean and Caribbean as they do in Europe.

The Court of Two Sisters is exemplary. It is L-shaped in the French manner, and built close to the street, the better to facilitate commerce. Creole merchants did business on the ground floor in the classic French manner; their families resided above. The extra-tall windows, doors, and the high ceilings and breezeways (or broad open galleries outside) promoted the flow of fresh air. In the atrium fashion of the Spanish, the house looked inward upon a verdant patio, ideal for alfresco family life, secluded and shadowed from the fierce rays of the sun.

The Vieux Carré was conceived along classic Renaissance lines. The old Place d'Armes was its signature, its grand centerpiece, overlooking the river. It was the perfect spot from which the French could overlook all river traffic, alien or familiar, military or commercial. Since New Orleans was overwhelmingly Roman Catholic, the major functions of both government and church were clustered close to one another, at the Place d'Armes (later renamed Jackson Square to honor the hero of the Battle of New Orleans, Andrew Jackson). The nation's oldest basilica, the St. Louis Cathedral, commanded the scene, flanked by the Cabildo (the seat of government) and the Presbytere (administrative headquarters for the Catholic church).

Since it was a crown colony long before the American Revolution, the streets were named with a shrewd sense of noblesse oblige and politesse. Rue Royale was the old city's main commercial thoroughfare, often referred to as "The Street of the Merchant Princes." Bourbon Street was named not for the whiskey but for the ruling French House of Bourbon. Like the decadent Royalists themselves, this once- swank dwelling place of aristocrats has fallen from grace.

Bourbon Street's overblown reputation for uninhibited revelry is a relatively recent phenomenon.

Rue Burgundy was named for the father of the boy king-apparent, the soon-to-become Louis XV. His regent, the Duc d'Orleans, an amoral opportunist, combined his talents for duplicity with John Law, a Scots schemer and financial swiftie, in such a way that the French Crown backed the venture—which history would call the "Mississippi Bubble"—peddling swampland real estate, while printing new money at such a furious pace it almost bankrupted La Belle France.

The Duke of Orleans was immortalized by having both a street and a city named after him. Law wisely saw to it that a St. Louis street honored his adolescent future king, but also that it separated the two royal bastards, a quarrelsome duo named Conti and Toulouse.

Governor Bienville took the cue, named himself a street (Bienville), and built his mansion on it. Today the boundary lines of the Vieux Carré remain the same—Iberville (named after Bienville's brother), the Mississippi River, Esplanade, and Rampart. Esplanade was the Public Commons, a broad, oak-shaded promenade where *les citoyens* could gallop their horses and show off their finery on Sunday afternoons. Rampart Street was named for the sagging, four-foot palisade, or rampart, that supposedly protected the colonists from invasion by hostile forces, red or white. It also supposedly protected them from the inconvenience of having their slaves escape the island of New Orleans.

New Orleans history endures vibrantly on every block in the French Quarter. It is more pageant than dull history. It is constant adventure and discovery.

You can see the oldest basilica in North America (the St. Louis Cathedral), the oldest building in the Mississippi Valley (the Ursuline convent), and the first town-house apartment buildings (the Pontalbas). It is the site of America's first grand opera house and its first pharmacy. It is the largest assembly of architecturally pure, historically authentic 19th-century buildings still standing in one compact downtown area—not recreations or replicas.

The Court of Two Sisters is one of those living landmarks. The distinctive Franco-Spanish courtyard is the most spacious and spectacular patio in the city, an embodiment of all that was gracious and romantic in Creole New Orleans. Encapsulated, it blooms year round, defying change.

Strolling Royal Street today you'll find, block upon block, the same crooked *banquettes* (sidewalks), the same gently sagging, over-hanging galleries (shelter from frequent rains), the louvered jalousies (shutters), the lush, green, sun-splashed patios offering solace from the clamor of the outside world. It is indeed another time, another place.

Over all, you'll find etched the abiding signature of *Nouvelle Orleans*: those unique traceries of iron grillwork known to natives as "iron lace." It ornaments the gates, the fences, and galleries of hundreds of French Quarter buildings, a mixture of the smith's sinew and the designer's delicacy.

French Quarter residents do not live *in* the past. They live *with* the past. History surrounds them, illuminates their lives, and makes them the richer for it. The citizens belong to no certain era, nationality, profession, or breed. They are writers, artists, merchants, restaurateurs, dealers in rare coins and stamps and priceless antiques, grocers, barkeeps, street entertainers, musicians, attorneys, physicians. Many have renovated old properties with love and respect. Native or transient, Orleanians share a certain feeling quite rare in our nation's fast-moving, technological, throwaway society. Call it what you will, it exudes a sense of perspective and place.

"Life is for the living," the old Creoles said. "If more of us knew how to live, there'd be fewer of us dead."

Street of the Merchant Princes

From the city's earliest days, Rue Royale has been Main Street. For two centuries, men and women of breeding and fashion have shopped on Royal, browsed, and sought bargains in fine furniture and tapestries, fine art, and jewelry. "The Street of Merchant Princes" remains much the same—a movable feast for shoppers seeking imported elegance, curios, and all kinds of exotica. It was in these small shops that the famed poet Eugene Field said he found "his greatest solace and delight" when he resided in the Vieux Carré.

Within a single stretch of seven city blocks there are 17 of the nation's major dealers in rare and certifiable antiques. Within a few blocks, centering on Royal, are located at least a dozen art galleries, both contemporary and period, exhibiting the work of established painters (many of whom reside and work in New Orleans).

Today's merchants include fourth- and fifth-generation families who have formed the Royal Street Art Guild. It exists for the same reason the guilds of Florence and Amsterdam and London were formed—to promote the arts and preserve tradition. They deal in masterpieces in jade and porcelain, 18th- through 20th-century European furniture and furnishings, Fabergé creations, priceless antiques, and rare weapons.

In the first block, at 116 Royal, the world-famous Sazerac cocktail was introduced in 1859. At 126 Royal, William Walker, the self-named "Grey-eyed Man of Destiny," was tried at the old U.S. District Court for "intervention in Nicaragua's internal affairs." Walker, an attorney and part-time soldier of fortune, defended himself, won acquittal, and invaded

19

Nicaragua again (for the fifth time). Wealthy American industrialists financed his band of mercenaries and, at one point, Walker ruled as El Presidente de Nicaragua for six months and was so recognized by President Franklin Pierce. Walker's career ended abruptly in 1860 before a Honduran firing squad. He was 36. Across the street (127 Royal), the building still stands where the oldest Carnival parading krewe, the Mystic Knights of Comus, was formed in 1857 above the Gem saloon.

At 301 Royal, the master furniture-maker of the antebellum South, Prudent Mallard, hand carved and sold the mahogany and rosewood chairs, armoires, and the magnificent four-poster beds that were the showpieces of Louisiana's classic plantation mansions. The same block contains the home of the first post office in the U.S. and the original Bank of Louisiana.

Farther down, at 413 Royal, was born Adrien Rouquette, the poet-priest and missionary to the Choctaw Indians. He became so attached to "the noble savages" that he took the Indian name of Chata-Ima ("He Who Is Like the Choctaw").

Four-seventeen is the boyhood home of Paul Morphy, the chess prodigy who was the first American to win the world championship. He won the title at the age of twenty-one and retired unbeaten at the age of twenty-two. Near the corner of Royal and St. Louis streets, the apothecary Anton Peychaud compounded his secret formula for mixing cognac and bitters in an eggcup (coquetier). It was conceived as a palliative to deaden pain. Following several coquetiers (and feeling little pain), his American clients translated "coquetier" into "cock-a-tail." That's how the modern "cocktail" got its name.

The posh Royal Orleans Hotel occupies the same site where the magnificent St. Louis Hotel once stood with its great domed rotunda, the jewel of Creole antebellum society.

Beneath its copper-plated, 100-ton canopy, slaves often were auctioned, Mardi Gras fashion, in various exotic costumes.

One of the oldest homes, 520 Royal, was built by Francois Seignouret, a native of Bordeaux and a designer-manufacturer of exquisite chairs and lounges. His initial "S," carved in fancy scroll, distinguished every piece he made. The building now houses the offices of WDSU, the city's first TV station. Its patio is among the most painted and photographed spots in the Vieux Carré.

At 529 Royal stands a Spanish structure, believed to have been the home of Don Estevan Miro, governor of Louisiana (1785-1791) when it was a colonial province of Spain. Within the next block, Rue Royale reaches its full glory. For this is the area known as "Governor's Row," a reminder that, of all 50 American states, Louisiana is the only one that once was a French (and Spanish) royal province. Here its residents lived, royally, for almost a century before New Orleans became a part of the United States.

Governor's Row

From its founding to the time of its transfer to the United States in 1803, a period of eighty-five years, *Nouvelle Orleans* was the capital of a French and later, a Spanish royal colony. Its governors were so far removed from their motherlands that it literally took six months to contact them by sailing ship. In effect, they were royal surrogates, almighty, endowed with the power of kings.

New Orleans enjoyed the status of a kind of independent island free state, a citadel of freebooting trade, surrounded by swamp and buffered by the huge Lake Pontchartrain and the nation's most powerful boulevard of commerce, the Mississippi. It was port of entry for half the American subcontinent, and the gateway to America's bounty. The world's treasures flowed freely through its portal.

"Governor's Row," the 600 block of Rue Royale, represented the political center of this Old World colony, and its Creole founders, the self-styled *"creme de la creme."* During the city's initial growth and transition to American domain, five governors lived in this particular block. A sixth governor resided half a block away. Two state Supreme Court justices owned homes in the 600 block. One future chief justice of the U.S. Supreme Court apprenticed here as a law clerk and later as an attorney.

Two New Orleans mayors resided on "Governor's Row," sharing that honor with a general who fought beside Andrew Jackson in the Battle of New Orleans, as well as a future president of the United States of America. "Governor's Row," the 600 block of Royal, remains one of the nation's most compact, historical, and architecturally distinct ensembles. History beckons from every gateway.

The Crawford House, 611 Royal, was built during the halcyon days of the 1830s when New Orleans was the fastest-growing city in America. This property once belonged to the Pontalba family, whose efforts to rebuild the Vieux Carré following two devastating fires are legendary. Micaela, the redoubtable "redheaded baroness," was responsible for the two historic "Pontalba" apartment houses that still flank Jackson Square.

The same site also was the home of Edward Grymes, the first American district attorney. A flexible fellow, Grymes resigned his office to become Jean Lafitte's lawyer when the buccaneer paid him $10,000 to spring his brother, Pierre Lafitte, from the calaboose. Grymes is said to have squandered the entire fee on one night of marathon gambling.

When Governor Claiborne placed a bounty on Jean Lafitte's head, Grymes interceded. Eventually, Lafitte and his "banditti" were offered pardon and American citizenship in return for their aid, and especially their vitally needed powder and flints, at the Battle of New Orleans. Ironically, Grymes bought the house on Royal Street . . . and then married Governor Claiborne's widow.

The distinctive twin homes at 612 and 624 Royal were built by the prominent Creole physician, Dr. Isidore Labatut, in 1831. They became the gathering places for the French Creole aristocracy, and the scenes of the more elegant Creole soirées.

Six twenty-four enjoys a special significance. It was there, in the house occupied by Dr. Labatut, that a young lawyer spent many nights poring over his books and notes. Edward Douglas White thus began an illustrious career that led him to the pinnacle of his profession: chief justice of the United States Supreme Court.

Jean Baptiste Labatut lived just across the street at 623

Royal. A prosperous merchant, Dr. Labatut's brother also practiced law and became attorney general of the Cabildo—the Spanish governing body before the Louisiana Purchase. Jean Baptiste was one Creole who thoroughly embraced the new American democracy. In 1815, he served with distinction as a general and aide-de-camp to Andrew Jackson on the field at Chalmette.

The lovely home next door, 621 Royal, dates back to 1825. It was, for a time, the residence of Zachary Taylor, before he became the twelfth president of the United States.

The modest, unassuming structure at 631 Royal is known as "Patti's Court." It is thought to be the second oldest structure on Rue Royale. The early history of the home is obscure, but notarial acts indicate that one Antoine Cavalier set up a mercantile establishment there in the 1780s. It was operated by his sons as late as 1809.

The celebrated teenage prima donna, Adeline Patti—"*le petite Patti*"—lived here in 1860 when she made her French Opera debut in "Lucia di Lammermoor." The French Opera House was newly opened and, as war clouds gathered, struggling to avoid bankruptcy. "The Divine Patti" was induced to cancel several concerts in an effort to save grand opera in New Orleans. The tiny diva gave 40 performances within a year. So sensational was her presence that both the French Opera House and the 18-year-old singer became permanent parts of local history and lore.

Directly across the street, at 628 Rue Royale, stands another ancient structure known as "The Royal Castilian Arms." It was the home of many French and Spanish Creole families during the final years of Spanish rule. No one knows the exact date of construction. It probably was built soon after the devastating fire that levelled most of the Vieux Carré in 1794. Adjoining it was the home of James Pitot, the first democratically elected mayor of American New Orleans (1804).

Royal Street was aptly named. Here resided the aristocracy of early New Orleans, the movers and shakers of Creole and antebellum New Orleans. It is not difficult to picture how it was. Near dusk, as the busy world mellows down, the odd-shaped iron lanterns flicker on. The coaches of the proud colonials rumble across the cobbled carriageways to deposit their elegantly attired passengers: the governor and his lady; the Spanish ambassador. The sensuous smells of night-blooming jasmine and sweet olive permeate the air. Huge torchlights (later gas lanterns) cast their eerie shadows. The patios, abloom always with foliage and the wild banana trees, are alive with music and laughter, perfectly convivial, another world.

Near the corner of 607 Royal lived His Honor Dennis Prieur, the only man to be elected mayor six times (1828-1843). Next door, at 609-611, the celebrated Creole Andre Bienvenu Roman resided. Roman was twice elected governor of Louisiana (1831-35, and 1839-43). (How unique. How convenient. The governor and the mayor living side by side for the better part of 12 years.)

Next door to them was the entrance to the most luxuriant patio of all, part of the colonial residences of two previous governors—613 Royal Street. Early in the eighteenth century, long before it became known as The Court of Two Sisters, this was the site of the mansion owned by Etienne de Perier Cenier. Perier was the second French colonial governor of the Royalist colony.

Between 1726 and 1733 he governed the infant province, besieged by flood and the threat of Indian war. Among his more notable achievements was the development of the levee system to keep the cantankerous Mississippi River from spilling over into the saucerlike city, six feet below sea level.

We have few clues as to what the governor's mansion looked

like. This building, along with more than 500 others (and many records), was destroyed by the great fire of 1794.

Perier was a nervous man, and with some reason. He governed at the time of the bloody Natchez Massacre of November 28, 1729. An estimated 700 of his countrymen, some of them relatives, were slaughtered by the Natchez Indian tribe at Fort Rosalie, where present-day Natchez, Mississippi commands the river's towering bluffs.

Almost everyone in New Orleans lost a relative or close friend. The Natchez took women, children, and slaves as prisoners. For one year, Governor Perier and his Choctaw allies chased the Natchez, recovering some prisoners, discovering some dead.

Finally, on November 15, 1730, Perier and an army of 650 soldiers and 350 Choctaw warriors set out to track them down once and for all, and trapped them at Black River, Louisiana. Perier brought back 427 Natchez prisoners, who were sent to Santo Domingo and sold as slaves. Virtually extinct, the tribe drifted into obscurity and eventually disappeared forever.

The Grand Marquis

New Orleans' first "Golden Age" began in May, 1743, with the arrival of a man so aristocratic and theatrical he was known for generations thereafter as the "The Grand Marquis." This highborn sophisticate's full name in itself was awe-inspiring: Pierre Cavagnal de Rigaud, Marquis de Vaudreuil. He immediately set about transforming this marshland frontier village into his "*petit Paris*"—Paris on the Big Muddy.

Vaudreuil brought with him all the elegance of manners and pretension that were the hallmark of Old World royalty. For 15 years, wherever he and his wife lived, the Grand Marquis presided over a constant round of elegant banquets, fêtes, promenades, costumed balls, and parties. They brought a shipload of expensive furniture with them from France and later imported the first "four-horse carriage" to New Orleans. He managed to not only introduce drama and Mardi Gras to the swamp, but also to establish standards of corruption and nepotism that became the hallmark of Louisiana politics.

There is still some confusion concerning exactly where the Grand Marquis presided over his "*petit Paris.*" The official governor's residence stood at the corner of Chartres and St. Ann. Yet the legends persist. In fact, as late as 60 years ago, local historian Allets Brazal wrote an extensive newspaper feature article declaring that the Grand Marquis occupied the house at 613 Royal Street at the time of his arrival. (Perhaps he later moved.)

Brazal's description of 613 Royal at the time of Vaudreuil's arrival in 1743 is too detailed to be lightly dismissed. The historian writes of the fine timbers of which the house was made and of a "secret preparation of cement mixture used to hold together the bricks."

Brazal further describes the ornate grillwork, the wrought-iron gate, the porte cochere (carriageway), even the cobblestone walks in the courtyard which were laid "in geometric patterns edged with purple violets." He specifically mentions the profusion of greenery—the banana trees, rare shrubs, peach, persimmon, pear, and fig trees from Cuba and Spain. "Night jasmine perfumed the air," Brazal concludes.

The tightly knit Creole community cheerily passed along both oral and written reminiscences of the Grand Marquis. In 1926, two descendants of the *creme de la creme*, Isabelle and Angelle Puig, regaled Meigs Frost, the *Picayune*'s sprightly roving reporter, with tales their forefathers told. The Puig family lived directly across from the Court, and they "always understood the Grand Marquis lived at 613 Royal."

Came a Cavelier

It was during Vaudreuil's Royalist regime that Mardi Gras was first celebrated. Charity hospital was built. Gambling was given free reign. And the systematic use of political "kickbacks" became a basic part of the French government.

According to charges filed by the King's "spies," the Grand Marquis personally profited from the sale of army provisions and cut himself a percentage of all trade monopolies. His wife allegedly struck up a partnership with the royal pharmacist and made a small fortune dealing illicit drugs.

Faced with exposure, the Grand Marquis beat his enemies to the punch. He issued a fiery proclamation denouncing corruption in *La Louisiane* and called for a thorough investigation. He and his spouse then departed for Canada, where his friend the king installed him as governor of that royal province—a most unusual punishment, to say the least.

Before leaving New Orleans, the Grand Marquis de Vaudreuil gave himself a truly royal sendoff. Two hundred of the city's Creole aristocrats attended a sumptuous farewell banquet. Champagne fountains overflowed with the bubbly. As a climax, two doves were released carrying lighted tapers in their beaks which were used to ignite a thunderous bombardment of fireworks that momentarily turned night into day.

Since almost every building in the Vieux Carré burned down at least once during the great firestorms of 1788 and 1794, historical gaps remain in our knowledge of the original colonial sites. History has been fuzzed over by mystery in many cases. Insufficient notarial records are available for many locations. So, the story persists that the man responsible for creating the

31

style and sophistication of old *Nouvelle Orleans*, the Paris of the Americas, did indeed once live at 613 Royal Street. Whether this was or was not in fact the case, today the Grand Marquis Room of The Court of Two Sisters, with its gourmet food, fine wines, and palatial decor, is a classic reminder of his eminence in this old Franco-Spanish city.

The present structure at 613-615 Royal Street, now known as The Court of Two Sisters, was constructed in the early 1830s during the city's first major economic boom. It was built for Jean Baptiste Zenon Cavelier, president of the Bank of New Orleans.

The Cavelier family was a strong presence on Governor's Row for over fifty years. Zenon Cavelier's father, Antoine, and his wife, Francoise, built the Spanish colonial city house that still stands just two doors away at 631 Royal. It served as the family home from the 1790s until the death of Antoine Cavelier, Jr., in 1850. Zenon, his wife Louise, and their five children lived upstairs at The Court of Two Sisters building, which was built in the French town house style, near the stores he and his brother operated at street level from both houses.

The Court of Two Sisters building passed out of the hands of the Cavelier family in 1854. Ownership, including the lease of the downstairs shop, was transferred twice during the turbulent years of "Yankee Occupation" and Reconstruction. Then, in 1886, it became the property of Emile Angaud, and a new shop opened on the ground floor. It was called "The Shop of the Two Sisters."

The Royal Street sign, a French Quarter landmark.

The famous Court of Two Sisters lantern lights the entrance on Bourbon Street.

The ornate Bourbon Street entrance gate is a fine example of the colonial ironsmith's art.

The Royal Court Room offers a romantic environment for a candlelight dinner.

A just-right table setting in the glass-enclosed gazebo.

The abundance of quality shines through at The Court of Two Sisters.

*At right, Traditional Creole dishes made with the freshest local ingredients are
highlighted at The Court of Two Sisters.*

Just a small portion of the tastes available at the sumptuous buffet.

The Court of Two Sisters offers the authentic tastes, sounds, and good times of New Orleans.

The Carriageway Bar offers visitors a restful atmosphere
in which to relax.

One of the best places in town to sample traditional New
Orleans concoctions: Sazerac, Court of Two Sisters
Toddy, Hurricane, Mint Julep, Brandy Milk Punch, and
Planters Punch.

A sign over the courtyard entrance inviting guests to experience the Creole traditions of fine food and warm hospitality.

An aerial view featuring the festive umbrellas of the courtyard of The Court of Two Sisters.

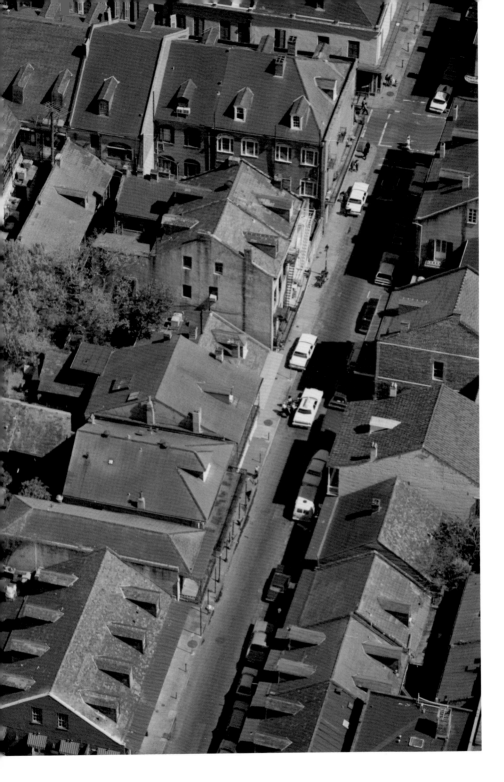

The Court of Two Sisters specializes in traditional Creole cuisine, served with a side of New Orleans atmosphere.

At right, The flavor of New Orleans is best experienced alfresco, in the largest and most historic courtyard in the French Quarter.

A strolling jazz trio brings the sounds of New Orleans to the courtyard.

The courtyard, with its quietly flowing fountain, was once the site of extravagant Creole parties.

A flaming dessert being prepared in The Court of Two Sisters' own traditional, dramatic style.

IN MEMORIAM
THE SISTERS, WHO OWNED
A FRENCH QUARTER SHOP WHICH
IS NOW IMMORTALIZED AS THE
COURT OF TWO SISTERS RESTAURANT
EMMA CAMORS MUSSO
BORN 1858, DIED OCT. 31, 1944
BERTHA CAMORS ANGAUD NOBLET
BORN 1860, DIED DEC. 19, 1944

The newly restored tomb of Emma and Bertha Camors, the sisters who gave The Court of Two Sisters its name.

The Two Sisters

The legendary "two sisters" for whom the courtyard at 613-615 Royal is named were born just prior to the Civil War, of distinguished Creole parentage. Emma (1858) and Bertha (1860) were said to be "as like as twins," even though two years apart. From the beginning they were extraordinarily close, even in death (they died the same year, 1944, within two months of each other, and are buried in the same family crypt at St. Louis Cemetery #3).

The "two sisters" were Creoles, descendants of the city's first settlers, cultured, educated, and proud. Like all true Creoles, Emma and Bertha grew up speaking fluent French as well as English.

They married, in close succession, French Creole men of substance, and lived in the Vieux Carré on Royal Street. Both sisters were widowed (Bertha twice), and thus it came to be that they opened a shop on the ground floor of the mansion at 613 Royal. It was what the French termed a "*rabais* shop," specializing in all sorts of "notions" of excellent quality, including ball dresses.

"The Shop of the Two Sisters," as they called it, became a distinctive part of the old French city. For twenty years (1886-1906) Emma and Bertha Camors (using their maiden names) sold handmade Carnival costumes, exquisite formal gowns during the Gay Nineties period, fine lace and novelties, perfumes, and the latest imports from France.

In the early 1900s Creole fortunes declined rapidly. Many of the "*creme de la creme*" were forced to move out of the old

French Quarter, causing the sisters' clientele to dwindle. Eventually, the two women were wrenched from their ancestral past by this change of fortune. They spent their last years sharing a modest half of a traditional shotgun house on North Dupre.

Bertha and Emma Camors left an indelible mark on the Vieux Carré, for the location forever would be known as The Court of Two Sisters. Descendants and friends of their neighbors fondly recall how Bertha and Emma, long after the death of Bertha's second husband, maintained an air of quiet dignity.

One lady, whose uncle married Bertha, recalls Sunday dinner with the two. "I was very young at the time, but I distinctly remember these two fine ladies, the sisters Camors. They dressed beautifully. They conversed brilliantly on a variety of subjects. They were, you might say, the epitome of the cultured Creole grand dame."

The two sisters were in their seventies when the Depression turned a good many lives upside down. Yet, Saturday nights, Bertha would play the piano, and Emma, who had studied voice in Europe, would sing. They still dressed impeccably, and neighbors recall how they would sit and talk for hours, sharing secret asides in French, while "dexterously knitting and performing fine crochet."

Oh, what grand stories they could tell. Bertha's second husband, Gaston Noblet, had once been known locally as "The Wizard." They loved to reminisce about his first animated Easter displays. Gaston also created magnificent scenery for the old French Opera House. But alas, the grand theater burned down in 1919, and with it the cultural-social center of French New Orleans disappeared.

And so, seldom separated, the two sisters—"alike as twins"—lived out their lives together, undaunted by loss of fortune, and died two months apart. The *Picayune* reported the death of Bertha on Christmas day, 1944, under the headline:

"TWO SISTERS NOW UNITED IN DEATH." The obituary read as follows:

New Orleans' famed "two sisters," for whom an old architectural gem was named in the Vieux Carré, were united in death today.

Mrs. Bertha Camors Noblet, 84 years old, died at her home, 1124 No. Dupre Street, and she was buried Wednesday with her sister in the family tomb at St. Louis Cemetery No. 3.

Her sister, Mrs. Emma Camors Musso, a constant companion and one-time co-owner with Mrs. Noblet of a variety shop at 613 Royal Street—now The Court of Two Sisters—died October 31 and was buried on All Saint's Day.

Natives of New Orleans, they were famous public figures until the turn of the century when the Vieux Carré was still the hub of much of the city's business and social activity. They retired in 1906.

The Court in Transition

The sisters had entered into business in 1886, not long after the purchase of the historic mansion and courtyard by Bertha's father-in-law, a wealthy merchant named Emile Angaud. When Angaud died in 1896, he left an estate that involved an inventory of 15 pieces of property, including the house and shops he leased at 613 Royal.

When Bertha's husband, Baldomero Angaud, passed on in 1904, the bulk of the estate descended through the sons of Baldomero's sister, Jeanne, to the del Valle family. Within two years, Bertha and sister Emma found it necessary to close their shop, unable to sustain their business at a time when the French Quarter was rapidly losing its Creole population in the wake of a flood of Italian immigration.

During the next three decades, the property at 613 Royal passed through seven ownerships. In 1925 it was purchased from the del Valle family heirs by Natalie Scott, one of New Orleans' most beloved writers and civic leaders. She held it for only one year. Times grew tougher and the French Quarter, run down and now quixotically Bohemian in nature, declined perceptibly. The Depression struck, leaving the proud Vieux Carré in a tattered state of transition and neglect.

Between 1925 and 1934, the sale value of The Court of Two Sisters declined from $39,000 to $14,000. There are no specific records, but the sisters' once elegant notion shop is said to have been, at various times, a small bistro, a refreshment stand, and, briefly, a speakeasy.

It remained for a young entrepreneur and super salesman named Jimmy Cooper to realize its full potential as a courtyard restaurant, capitalizing on the romance and mystique of the site. In 1940, he opened The Court of Two Sisters restaurant and ran it until his death on New Year's Eve, 1956.

Despite the limited size of the building's downstairs kitchen, Cooper developed a lively tourist trade, enhanced by the flow of servicemen and women from all over the nation during the wartime years when New Orleans was a major shipbuilding and embarkation center. Cooper offered his visiting patrons food, entertainment, and romance at moderate prices—a memorable respite from the grim realities of war and for many young couples a trysting place in the heart of charming old New Orleans.

Cooper was wise enough to realize that, while the appeal to tourists would build his national reputation, he must also appeal to local families and the younger generation as well. At a time when many Orleanians shunned the Quarter, wary of its dark "Bohemian influence," young people soon were taking their dates to the Court without discouragement from their parents.

Jimmy Cooper was a showman. At one time, he presented opera in the huge courtyard. It wasn't a frivolous idea, really. The first permanent opera company in the U.S. was established just two blocks away on St. Ann Street in 1808.

In 1947, Cooper added two additional parcels of land, 612 and 620 Bourbon Street, not only expanding the operation but affording it entrances on both Bourbon and Royal. When he died in 1956, however, the Court almost went to seed. It drastically needed someone with Cooper's flair—plus the management skills to fully develop its restaurant potential.

A Fein Romance

Joe Fein was, by acclamation of his peers, unique in the highly competitive New Orleans restaurant business. Admittedly lacking "kitchen experience" in a city once dominated by old-line restaurant families, he took the dormant Court of Two Sisters in 1963 and within eight years completely restored the building, its historic ambiance . . . and its proud reputation.

Fein was anything but inexperienced in the food industry. He had built a highly successful, diversified food service business, Jos. Fein Caterer, Inc. In 1956, "having fallen in love with the business," he bought Gluck's, an established, highly regarded restaurant on Royal Street.

Three years later, Gluck's burned down.

"It was a tragedy," Joe Fein recalled. "But those years with Sam Gluck taught me a lot about the food business. One thing in particular . . . there's a big difference between fresh and frozen fish. In fact, food in New Orleans begins with 'fresh.'"

So Joe Fein started fresh by buying and restoring The Court of Two Sisters. By the time he was finished, it was a classic French Quarter renovation with greatly increased kitchen and dining facilities, able to accommodate up to 1,000 patrons— 600 in the courtyard itself.

He pumped a small fortune into the Court. "We wanted to make it like it was. Give it the character it deserved. Make it blend with the Quarter."

The Gazebo, an indoor dining room, was made from part of the patio as a pleasant sanctuary during inclement weather. The second and third stories, previously used for storage, were converted into spacious kitchens, offices, and special banquet rooms.

"People should come here not just to eat," Joe Fein declared, "but for the history and charm of it. New Orleans is one of the world's most romantic cities. The Court reflects this." Then he told a reporter with a wink, "You know, there's a legend locally that more proposals of marriage have been made here than anywhere in the country."

Joe Fein, whose sons now carry on the tradition, was a dynamic part of the renewal of the French Quarter and its vastly expanded tourist trade. Fein was a co-founder of the annual New Orleans Food Festival. He chaired the national convention of the Food Service Executives Association. In 1967 he received the group's coveted Culinary Arts Award.

An active member of the New Orleans Tourist Commission and the Super Bowl Task Force, he became deeply involved in restaurant promotion locally, regionally, and nationally. He was elected by his peers as president of the New Orleans Restaurant Association and later the Louisiana Restaurant Association.

Today his sons, Jerome and Joe Fein III, who grew up working in the restaurant, speak proudly of their father's vision: of what food should be, and what New Orleans symbolizes. The family romance with the Two Sisters carries on. Where else, they ask, can you linger and bask in the history and charm of two centuries of European tradition . . . touch a "charmed gate" wrought for an emperor . . . behold an ancient "wishing well" . . . and discover the ten flags, displayed in the old carriageway, that flew at various times over this cosmopolitan city?

Some even say the ghost of the voodoo queen Marie Laveau and the pirate-patriot Jean Lafitte still stalk the courtyard where the smell of jasmine and sweet olive are, in themselves, timeless and intoxicating. Who are we to say it isn't true?

A Visual Feast

In this old French Creole city, the patio (or courtyard) was absolutely essential. It was a refuge from the outside world, an oasis of family living, serene and ever green. The Court of Two Sisters exemplifies the wisdom of its early residents. This is the most spacious of all French Quarter patios, situated in the very "*coeur du Vieux Carré*" (the heart of the French Quarter).

If New Orleans is a banquet for all the senses, The Court of Two Sisters is a visual feast. Here you can sit in the comforting embrace of eternal spring, order a Sazerac or a mint julep, relax, and allow your imagination full play.

The patio is alive with lush foliage, including banana trees, Spanish bayonets, and a spectacular weeping willow. One section used to be enclosed with ornate iron lace work, and generations have danced upon its marble floor.

A genuine, down-home New Orleans jazz band performs regularly for diners and those who drop in to unwind and sip from a variety of libations. The old fountain cheerfully bubbles away, adding to the tranquility of the Old World atmosphere.

The Charm Gates at the carriage entrance, legend has it, were wrought in Spain for Emperor Maximillian of Mexico. Legends die hard in New Orleans. So, if indeed these gates found their way to the portal of 613 Royal, we assume the grateful sisters, Bertha and Emma Camors, surely considered them "charmed." At any rate, generations of visitors have touched them, hoping to carry away a bit of the grace that endures in this magical courtyard.

Stroll through the carriageway arch and you'll see displayed the ten sovereign flags that have flown over Louisiana. These include the flags of France (twice), England, Spain, (twice), Louisiana (between secession and being in the Confederacy), the Confederate States of America, the United States (twice), plus that rambunctious 45-day wonder, the Republic of West Florida. The latter came about because of the fact that, following the Louisiana Purchase, citizens of the so-called Florida parishes were still under Spanish rule. In 1810 they declared their independence and invited the U.S. to annex them. This Bonnie Blue flag with a lone star preceded the Texas flag by 25 years.

New Orleans' exotic history is so animated with larger-than-life incidents and characters that it is difficult at times to separate fact from fiction. For example, near the celebrated arbor trellis in the courtyard is a normal wishing well. However, local legend-makers, spellbound by the recondite mysteries of voodoo, could not leave well enough alone. They renamed it the Devil's Wishing Well, based on the supposition that since Marie Laveau, the very real Voodoo Queen of New Orleans, lived but a few blocks away, she most certainly must have practiced her orgiastic voodoo rites in the torchlit confines of the city's largest patio.

Orleanians, ever eager to embellish the tallest of tales, took to casting coins into the well for good luck. Then they had a drink or two—absinthe was once a local favorite, a devilish drink known to drive men crazy—and spun other yarns, fancified or fanciful, inspired by a combination of strong drink and vigorous imagination.

One such tale involves the so-called "gentleman-pirate" Jean Lafitte. Local myth-makers delight in telling how the buccaneer dispatched three men in a single duel on the courtyard floor. In point of fact, Lafitte is not known to have ever unsheathed his sword in anger. The "Bos" was CEO of a privateer operation on Bayou Barataria, spoke five languages, sold contraband goods to New Orleans' finest, and employed 1,000 men of varying dispositions, "cutthroat to professional mercenary," to do his fighting for him.

C'est la vie. If there is anything that is capable of scaring up the spirits of legendary past heroes (especially rascals), it is surely the *spiritus fermenti.* Lafitte did in fact own a blacksmith shop not far from 613 Royal which he used as a cover for his smuggling operations. He settled his conflicts with the establishment through his attorney, John Grymes, who resided just two doors away from the courtyard's entrance.

Nevertheless, the legends persist. Lafitte, the old-timers say, is buried in everybody's backyard, and so is his ill-gotten booty. Undoubtedly, the rogue managed to stash away at least a few doubloons underneath The Court of Two Sisters. Similarly, according to the tellers of tales there is not a block in the French Quarter where Marie Laveau did not perform some satanic rite. In truth, she specialized in potions and powders and "consultation" sessions with well-heeled white townsfolk, dispensing eerily accurate personal information, some of which was based on her network of slave informers. She died a penitent, was given a proper Roman Catholic burial, and is entombed in St. Louis Cemetery #1.

In the realm of reality, one of the Court's true treasures is an antique, coal-burning stove decorated with hand-carved brass figurines, which was the possession of the two sisters, Bertha and Emma Camors.

Dining and Celebration

"We may live without friends, we may live without books;
But civilized man cannot live without cooks.
He may live without love—what is passion but pining?
But where is the man who can live without dining?"

Bulwer Lytton

The late Joe Fein believed that, just as fine wine must be served at the proper temperature, fine dining was impossible without the proper atmosphere. The Fein family has enhanced that atmosphere with a variety of dining alternatives. In recent years, the Court has emerged as the place for a daily jazz brunch.

"We're so crowded," Jerome Fein says, "with both locals and visitors that we can't always handle everyone. The Court serves Sunday brunch every day. There are ninety different items on the buffet table, any fresh seafood that's in season, plenty of salads, and omelettes made to order."

For those who prefer the modern convenience of controlled temperature and humidity, winter or summer, there is the Royal Court Room. It offers all the comforts of twentieth-century living in an old-fashioned setting—brick walls and greenery. Another alternative to the courtyard is the Grand Marquis Room, named in honor of the elegant French governor. This room offers palatial decor, gourmet food, and superb wines. The Grand Marquis would have been pleased.

The Gazebo Room is known as the "Outside-In" room. Air-conditioned, it overlooks the lush, semi-tropical courtyard in

61

picture-window splendor. It invites those not fully accustomed to New Orleans' humid weather to relax, enjoy the scenery, and literally dine outdoors inside.

"The stomach is the only part of man that can be fully satisfied," Thomas Edison said, "yet never satisfied fully." For that reason, Creole cooking is a continually evolving art.

"New Orleans Creole cuisine," says Jerome Fein, "evolved from many sources and it continues to grow. Like jazz, it was not invented; it grew gradually."

All of which leads us to the essence of this book: Creole cooking, and how you can do some yourself.

"What is Creole?"

Next to the queries "Where is the French Quarter?" and "How do I find Bourbon Street?" the question most often asked by visitors to New Orleans is: "What is Creole?"

The word is derived from the Spanish term "*criollo*" or "a child born in the colonies." Originally, it referred to any person of European descent born in Spanish America or the West Indies.

In New Orleans, it was applied definitively to those descended from the original French or Spanish settlers. Today, Creole survives not so much as a race or breed as it does as an attitude, a way of living rooted mainly in the city's Gallic heritage.

The original Creoles thought of themselves as French and called themselves French well into the 1800s. They imported French wines, French books, French clothes. Their children, if possible, were educated in Paris. Even as their fortunes declined and those late-comers, the upstart "Américains," took control of the city, many stubbornly continued to speak French, adhere to French customs, and even refuse to speak English.

The Creole French were proud, independent people who called themselves "*la creme de la creme.*" They believed there was an art to everything in life and it began with the art of living.

Creoles established grand opera in America. They introduced Mardi Gras and the dice game known as "craps." They concocted the first "cocktail" and gave us that gustatory marvel, Creole cuisine. They of course claimed it was the highest form of cooking. "Creole" denoted "biggest, richest, best." Creole cabbages were succulent beyond compare. Creole gumbo was an unmatched melange of herbs and spices and seafood (and sometimes sausage and sometimes chicken, no two gumbos quite alike).

Use of the term "Creole" grew as the French found success in advertising their products as distinctive from the Americans'. "Creole" implied native-grown, therefore superior. As competition increased, Creole was applied to almost everything: Creole tomatoes (bigger and meatier), Creole corn (tastier, more tender), Creole horses (sleeker, faster).

The Creole stamp was on everything. If not, the Creoles (though greatly outnumbered) magically absorbed what they desired and ignored the rest. When a "foreigner" married into the family, he became Creole. Thus, an Irishman named O'Brien was transformed into an Obreon. A German named Zweig (meaning "branch") fostered a new branch of the family tree, surnamed LaBranche.

So, what is Creole? Gaggling over definitions seems useless— a kind of futile shadowboxing with the past. Best let it be said that, in New Orleans, almost everyone has been happily "Creolized" for some time. *Bon appétit.*

Part 2: The Recipes

Introduction to Cookbook Section

The eminent English writer, William Makepeace Thackeray, visited New Orleans in 1887 and came away singing the praises of New Orleans cuisine. "This old Franco-Spanish city, of all the cities in the world," he said, "is the city where you can eat the most and suffer the least, where the claret is as good as Bordeaux, and where the ragout and a bouillabaise can be the like of which you have never eaten in Paris or Marseilles."

Mark Twain, in his own impish way, commented, "Creole cooking is as delicious as the less criminal forms of sin."

Creole cooking begins, in most cases, with a recipe in itself, the time honored refrain: "First you begin with a roux . . ."

The roux is generally a blend of butter and flour, stirred constantly in an iron pot over a low fire until light brown in color. Approximately four tablespoons of butter with one cup of flour are incorporated. Ultimately, chopped onions, bell pepper, parsley, garlic, celery, and a variety of herbs and spices may be introduced to enhance the flavor of the dish you are preparing. The roux was the basis for virtually all Creole dishes involving fish or meat.

Today, there is some confusion between Creole and Cajun cuisine. The Creoles were essentially townspeople, urban and sophisticated, who grew up influenced by Paris.

The Cajuns, on the other hand, were relatively unsophisticated, rural French migrants from Nova Scotia. They grew up isolated in a lowland swampy area crisscrossed by bayous, and lived off the land, the sea, and inland waters.

Both cultures savored good food and were adventuresome in its preparation, especially in the art of "stretching" foodstuffs, enhancing leftovers, and using spices and herbs to arouse the palate. Neither cuisine was really French. There were too many Spanish, Indian, and African-American (or Caribbean) influences.

Creole cooking was not invented. It evolved, much as that other indigenous art form called jazz, a mixture of many ethnic sources. First there was the French love of, and skill in, "manipulating anything edible into a tasty dish." To this was added the Spanish zest for piquancy, a certain spiciness. To these were added the African talent for slow-cooking to perfection and the seasonings—the herbs and spices of the Choctaw and Chickasaw Indians.

The recipes you will find in this book reflect a cross section of New Orleans cooking, Creole-inspired and time- and taste-tested by the discriminating palates of tens of thousands of customers. Feedback from the Court's customers is a special ingredient in continually rating the cuisine. Every table has a comment card for the guests to fill out. Jerry and Joe Fein read every single one each night.

It should be noted that a true variety of herbs and spices find their way into many recipes. It seems impossible for a New Orleans cook to live without them, and equally impossible for a New Orleans cook to measure them (except by instinct or memory). The old Creoles had a saying for this: "May lightning strike very soon the cook who measures herbs by the tablespoon." Unfortunately, this type of feel for Creole cooking takes years of experience to develop, so measurements are indicated. You'll just have to take your chances with the lightning.

Herbal cooking is almost as old as the city. An enterprising woman, Sister Xavier, arrived with the first group of Ursuline nuns in 1727 to open a school and hospital. She is recognized today as the first woman pharmacist in the New World. Locally, due to an absence of licensed physicians, she was the nearest thing to a doctor in colonial New Orleans.

Sister Xavier negotiated a large plot of land, an herb garden, where she grew an amazing assortment of plants used first as medicines and palliatives and secondly as seasonings. Chives, for example, were rich in sulphur and a remedy for bleeding. Basil was considered fundamental for the development of a "happy heart." Garlic was excellent for improving the flow of blood and facilitated good digestion.

"A happy heart" was essential to good health . . . and proper eating. For the further improvement of one's blood flow and sense of well-being, wine was the necessary lubricant to make one optimistic and sanguine and garlic the extra touch in the elevation of eating to the status of fine dining. The Creoles had a saying for all of that, too.

> "Celui que bonde, mange de boudin."
> ("He who sulks, eats his own stomach.")

So, with a "happy heart," and a proper sense of adventure, we invite you to sample this authentic experience in genuine New Orleans cooking. If you haven't sampled Creole food before, you stand to be pleasantly surprised. For nothing you've eaten before can possibly compare.

Creole chefs were fond of toasting each other by declaring over a glass of Bordeaux, "May the greatest dishes of the past be the sorriest dishes of the future!"

Bon Appétit!

Drinks

Eye Openers

Every day is a day of celebration at The Court of Two Sisters, where the party always begins before brunch with an opener— eye openers, we call them. Here is a group of New Orleans originals and, among them, our own personal favorites.

SAZERAC COCKTAIL

> 1¾ oz. rye whiskey
> ½ oz. simple syrup (2 tsp.
>   sugar, dissolved in water)
> 3 dashes Angostura bitters
> 3 dashes Peychauds bitters
> anisette liqueur
> lemon twist
> cracked ice

Place whiskey, syrup, and bitters into a cocktail shaker with cracked ice, shake briefly until chilled, and strain into an old-fashioned glass that has been thinly coated with Herbsaint or another anisette liqueur (such as Pernod). Add a lemon twist. Dazzling!

GONE WITH THE WIND

> 1 oz. vodka
> 1 oz. Mandarin Napoleon
> cracked ice

Chill well in cracked ice, strain, and serve up in a martini glass.

PLANTER'S PUNCH

A drink worth serving to a crowd—so we've included the recipe for a half gallon of punch base.

> 8 oz. pineapple juice
> 8 oz. orange juice
> 4 oz. grapefruit juice
> 8 oz. cherry juice
> 32 oz. lemon sour mix
> 4 oz. grenadine

For each cocktail combine 2 oz. of the above Planter's Punch Mix in a tall glass with:
> 2 oz. Appleton or Mount Gay rum
> a splash of red table wine
> 1 orange slice
> 1 cherry
> 1 pineapple cube

MINT JULEP

> 2 oz. bourbon
> ½ oz. simple syrup (2 tsp.
>   sugar, dissolved in water)
> 6-8 mint leaves
> 1 mint sprig
> 1 orange slice
> 1 cherry
> crushed ice

In a balloon glass crush 6-8 mint leaves with a spoon. Fill with crushed ice, then pour bourbon and syrup over ice. Garnish with a sprig of mint, orange slice, and cherry.

NEW ORLEANS GIN FIZZ

10 oz. gin
4 oz. simple syrup (2 tsp. sugar,
    dissolved in water)
2 oz. lemon sour mix
½ oz. orange flower water
    (available at liquor stores)
1 egg white
8 oz. milk
4 oz. half-and-half
crushed ice

Combine all ingredients but ice in a blender and blend on high speed until frothy. Serve over crushed ice. Best by the pitcher.

TWO SISTERS TODDY

½ oz. strawberry liqueur
½ oz. Grand Marnier
1 oz. bourbon
crushed ice
lemon twist

Combine all ingredients in a blender and blend until smooth. Serve up in a champagne glass garnished with a twist of lemon.

CAFE MIKE FEIN

6 oz. hot black coffee
1½ oz. Cognac
French vanilla ice cream
whipped cream

Pour coffee and Cognac into a tall coffee mug. Top with a small scoop of French vanilla ice cream and whipped cream.

Salads

On the lighter side of The Court of Two Sisters' menu are the wonderful salads presented each day at Jazz Brunch, iced down in a large piroque (or Cajun canoe) at the back of the restaurant, right at the edge of the courtyard.

TWO SISTERS' CHICKEN SALAD

3 cups cooked chicken, diced
1 cup celery, thinly sliced
½ cup onions, minced
1 tsp. salt
2 tbs. lemon juice
1 cup seedless grapes, sliced
¼ cup mayonnaise
11 oz. can mandarin oranges,
   drained
½ cup toasted almonds
Romaine or Boston lettuce

Since a small, cooked fryer will yield three to four cups of diced meat, use the entire chicken for this recipe, even if it runs a bit over. In a large salad bowl blend together chicken, celery, onions, salt, lemon juice, and grapes and refrigerate well. Just prior to serving add mayonnaise, oranges, and almonds, tossing gently to avoid breaking the oranges. Serve on leaves of Romaine or Boston lettuce or scoop generously into an avocado half. Serves 4 large portions or 8 small portions.

CAJUN PASTA SALAD

> 1 lb. elbow pasta
> 1 lb. smoked sausage
> ½ cup red peppers
> 2 bell peppers, diced
> 1 tbs. garlic, pureed
> 2 stalks celery, diced
> ½ white onion, diced
> 2 tbs. Toulouse seasoning
>   (see below)
> 2 bay leaves
> 1 tbs. Creole mustard
> ¼ cup white vinegar
> ¾ cup salad oil
> ¼ cup parsley

Cook the pasta in gently boiling water until *al dente*. Remove from heat, drain, rinse, and cool. Combine all ingredients in a large bowl. Toulouse seasoning is a combination of salt, white pepper, black pepper, onion powder, cayenne pepper, paprika, and thyme in equal amounts of one tablespoon each. You may also wish to sauté the sausage briefly before adding. The dish is best served at room temperature; however, chill thoroughly if preparing ahead of time and allow to stand one hour before serving. Serves 6 large portions or 12 small portions.

SPICY SHRIMP SALAD

> 2 lbs. cooked and shelled
>   gumbo shrimp
> ½ cup celery, diced
> ½ cup red onions, diced
> 1-3 stalks green onions, diced
> ⅓ cup mayonnaise

⅓ cup Creole mustard
½ tsp. salt
½ tsp. Tabasco sauce

Combine all ingredients in a large salad bowl and blend together until well covered by mayonnaise and mustard. Serve chilled on a bed of lettuce or use to stuff an avocado or tomato. Serves 4 large portions or 8 small portions.

PASTA AND CRAWFISH

1½ lb. Rotelle pasta
½ lb. mozzarella cheese, cubed
1 lb. crawfish tails, cooked
¼ cup fresh jalapeño peppers,
    seeded and diced
¼ bag torn spinach

Cook pasta in six to eight quarts of boiling water until al dente. Drain and toss with remaining ingredients and parmesan dressing (below). Serves 8.

Parmesan Dressing

1 egg
1 cup salad oil
½ cup Parmesan cheese, grated
¼ cup white wine vinegar
½ tsp. white pepper
½ tsp. salt
¼ tsp. ground cloves
1 tsp. garlic, minced

Place egg in food processor and mix, adding oil in a thin stream until thick. Add cheese, vinegar, and seasonings, blending until smooth.

CAESAR SALAD

A classic Caesar salad adds romance to any dinner, especially here at The Court of Two Sisters, where it is prepared by our waiters tableside. The dressing is at once tart and pungent, the salad texture crispy and crunchy from the combination of Romaine and fresh croutons. The recipe below serves 2. For more, simply multiply the ingredients for the desired quantity.

> 1 small head Romaine lettuce,
>   washed and drained
> 1 cup croutons
> 1 lemon
> 2 to 3 cloves garlic
> 1 tbs. Dijon mustard
> 2 fillets of anchovies
> 1 coddled egg
> 1 tbs. Worcestershire sauce
> 1 cup extra virgin olive oil
> ½ cup balsamic vinegar
> 1 tsp. salt
> ½ tsp. ground black pepper
> ⅓ cup Parmesan cheese

Into a large, well-seasoned wooden salad bowl squeeze the juice of one lemon, removing the seeds. Add the anchovies, crushing with a fork until a paste begins to form. Repeat for the garlic. Then add mustard and Worcestershire and blend well. Mix in the coddled egg (slightly warmed, not boiled) using a whisking motion with a fork until smooth. Continue whipping as you drizzle in the olive oil, then blend in the vinegar, salt, and freshly ground pepper. Toss with Romaine leaves torn into bite-size pieces, add croutons and Parmesan, and toss again until lettuce is well covered. Serve onto chilled salad plates and top with extra ground pepper.

CEVICHE

This is an exciting cold fish salad. Don't let the raw fish fool you; the marinade cooks the fish chemically and completely.

**4 lbs. red drum or any thick-textured fish such as amberjack, uncooked
1 large white onion, sliced
2 large bell peppers, sliced
3 limes, sliced thinly
1 small jar diced pimentos, drained
1¼ cups jalapeños, sliced
2 tbs. garlic, diced
4 scallions, chopped
1½ tbs. Tabasco sauce
1½ cups white wine vinegar
1½ cups white wine
¾ cup virgin olive oil
1 cup sugar
1 tbs. black peppercorns
1½ tsp. dried basil
1½ tsp. dried oregano
1 tbs. salt
½ stalk celery, chopped**

Slice fish into 1½" pieces. Mix together all ingredients and gently toss with fish to combine. Refrigerate and allow to marinate 24 hours. Serve cold. Serves 6 large portions or 12 small portions.

HOUSE SALAD DRESSING

In typical French Quarter fashion, even salad dressings are livelier and spicier than the norm. The Court of Two Sisters' house salad dressing offers a hearty, pungent contrast, especially to more bitter seasonal greens. Nicknamed "Royal Street Russian" by its tongue-in-cheek devotees, you may find it your home favorite, too.

> **3 cups French dressing (see**
> **recipe below)**
> **3 boiled eggs**
> **2 oz. anchovy paste**
> **5 oz. blue cheese**
> **1 oz. Lea & Perrin Sauce**

Cut or crumble eggs and cheese. Fold in the remainder of the ingredients. Hold chilled for service. Yields 1 quart.

French Dressing

> **3 cups mayonnaise**
> **⅓ cup white vinegar**
> **½ tsp. garlic, pureed**
> **½ tbs. paprika**
> **1 oz. sugar**
> **salt to taste**
> **white pepper to taste**

Mix all ingredients well and refrigerate.

Sauces

Sauces for Shrimp

There are two classic sauces for shrimp appetizers served at The Court of Two Sisters: the ever-popular cocktail sauce and the New Orleans original, remoulade sauce. Our renditions are enclosed herewith:

CLASSIC COCKTAIL SAUCE

>1 cup catsup
>2 tbs. prepared horseradish
>2 tbs. Worcestershire sauce
>1 tbs. lemon juice
>1 tsp. pepper
>1 dash salt

Whisk all ingredients together in a large bowl and refrigerate well. Serve liberally with six to eight boiled jumbo shrimp for appetizers or centered at the table for a peel 'em and eat 'em fest. Yields 1¼ cups.

REMOULADE SAUCE

>2 cups Creole mustard
>4 tbs. celery, diced
>4 stalks green onions, chopped
>2 tbs. parsley, chopped
>1 tbs. paprika
>⅓ cup salad oil
>¼ cup white wine vinegar
>4 tbs. garlic, pureed

1 dash salt
3 tbs. prepared horseradish
1 tbs. Worcestershire sauce
lettuce

In a mixer or blender combine all ingredients and blend until smooth. Chill completely. Serve over boiled medium shrimp arranged on a bed of shredded lettuce. Yields 3 cups.

More Sauces

TARTAR SAUCE

1 cup mayonnaise
½ cup dill pickle relish
2 tbs. scallions, diced
½ tsp. salt
¼ tsp. black pepper
¼ tsp. garlic salt

Combine ingredients in a large mixing bowl and whisk together. Chill and serve as a condiment with any seafood dish. Works especially well with fried shellfish. Yields 1½ cups.

SAUCE MAISON

1 cup mayonnaise
⅓ cup Creole mustard (or any
    whole-grained mustard)
1½ tsp. lemon juice
¼ cup scallions, chopped
1 dash Worcestershire sauce

1 dash cayenne pepper
½ tsp. Tabasco sauce

Mix ingredients well and serve with boiled shrimp. Yields 2 cups.

SAUCE ROYAL COURT

A fetching sauce served over fettucine, rigatoni, or any other type of pasta.

¼ cup flour
2 tbs. margarine
1 can artichoke bottoms,
   drained
1½ tsp. lemon juice
⅔ cup sliced mushrooms
¼ cup sherry
1 cup chicken stock
½ cup sliced black olives, sliced
1 bay leaf
⅓ cup scallions, chopped
3 tbs. parsley, chopped
1 tsp. onion salt
1 tsp. white pepper
¾ tsp. rosemary, crushed
½ tsp. thyme, crushed
½ cup heavy cream

Melt margarine and whisk in flour. Sauté mushrooms briefly, then add olives and seasonings. Pour in chicken stock and bring to a boil until thickened slightly. Reduce heat and add artichokes, sherry, scallions, parsley, and lemon juice. Allow to simmer ten minutes. Add cream, mixing well, and remove from heat. Yields 1 quart.

MOULIN ROUGE DIP

> 1 cup unsweetened whipped
>   cream
> 2 tbs. sour cream
> 1½ tsp. cayenne pepper
> ¾ cup chili sauce
> 1 tbs. chives, chopped
> 1½ tsp. Italian seasoning
> 3 tbs. Worcestershire sauce

Mix well and serve centered in a profusion of raw vegetables.
Yields 2 cups.

MUSTARD DIP

> 1 cup mayonnaise
> ½ cup prepared mustard
> 1 tsp. cayenne pepper
> ¾ cup sour cream
> ½ cup prepared horseradish
> 1 dash salt

Mix together and chill. Serve centered in fresh vegetables.
Yields 3 cups.

Soups

TURTLE SOUP

    1 lb. turtle meat
    1½ tbs. garlic, pureed
    ¾ cup white onion, diced
    ¾ cup celery, diced
    1 bell pepper, diced
    1 cup margarine
    1½ cups flour
    1 tomato, peeled and diced
    3 tbs. parsley, chopped
    6 qts. water
    3 hard boiled eggs
    1 tsp. lemon juice
    ¼ tsp. lemon peel, grated
    2 tbs. Worcestershire sauce
    1 tbs. Tabasco sauce
    2 tbs. salt
    1 bay leaf
    1 tsp. black pepper
    1 pinch thyme
    1 pinch oregano
    4 cubes beef bouillon
    3 tbs. Kitchen Bouquet
    sherry

Combine flour and margarine in a stockpot and create a roux by heating margarine until smoking or sizzling and then gradually adding flour and stirring mixture for 15-20 minutes until nut brown. Do not allow mixture to darken too fast. Add seasonings and vegetables and sauté until tender. Heat water, add bouillon cubes, stir, and add to roux. Chop turtle meat and eggs, combine with lemon peel, and set aside. Add tomato, parsley, and lemon juice to soup with Worcestershire, Tabasco, and Kitchen Bouquet. Blend in turtle mixture and cook on slow boil for 45 minutes. Garnish with a dash of sherry. Yields 2 gallons.

SEAFOOD GUMBO

1 cup celery, diced
1 cup bell pepper, diced
1 cup white onion, diced
2 cups okra, sliced
1½ tsp. pureed garlic or garlic paste
1 cup margarine or cooking oil
1½ cups flour
¼ cup parsley, chopped
1½ lbs. small or medium shrimp, peeled
6 qts. water
4 scallions, chopped
1½ lbs. gumbo crabs
2 tomatoes, peeled and chopped
1 pint oysters
1 tsp. thyme
1 tsp. basil
1 bay leaf, crushed
2 tbs. salt
1½ tsp. cayenne pepper
1 tsp. black pepper
2 tbs. Kitchen Bouquet
rice

In a large stockpot make a medium dark roux of the flour and margarine, heating the margarine until it is sizzling and gradually adding the flour and darkening. Add seasonings and vegetables, cook until vegetables are limp, and let cool about a half an hour. Boil shrimp separately, reserving stock. Add roux and vegetables to stock and blend well until thickened. Add oysters, crab, shrimp, and Kitchen Bouquet for color. Simmer one-half hour. Serve over rice. Yields 2 gallons.

CHICKEN & ANDOUILLE GUMBO

Gumbo, quite literally the bouillabaisse of Louisiana Creole cuisine, takes on many dimensions in the stockpot, from a rich complement of available seafoods to a more land-locked version featuring the always available chicken and the inimitable native smoked sausage, andouille. This particular Court of Two Sisters gumbo recipe keeps New Orleanians and would-be New Orleanians flocking back to its Royal Street courtyard for starters to a classic Creole luncheon or dinner.

> 3 cups diced white onions, plus
>   one quartered
> 2 cups bell pepper, diced
> 2 cups diced celery, plus one
>   stalk
> 1 clove garlic, minced
> 3 cups flour
> 1 lb. margarine or 1 cup of oil
> 1½ tsp. thyme
> 1 bay leaf
> 1 tsp. ground cloves
> 1½ tsp. cayenne pepper
> 1 tsp. basil
> 4 tbs. salt

1½ tsp. black pepper
3-4 green onions, diced
1 lb. andouille sausage
1 2½ to 3 lb. chicken,
    quartered
1½ gallons water
white or brown rice
diced scallions or minced
    parsley

Quarter and cook chicken on low boil covered with 6 quarts water in a heavy stockpot, adding one quartered white onion and one celery stalk, for 1 to 1½ hours. Drain and cool chicken, preserving the stock. Pick chicken clean, discarding skin and bones, and set meat aside. Separately dice and cook andouille sausage in a skillet, drain completely, and set aside. Finely dice all vegetables.

In a large skillet, heat margarine or oil over medium high heat, slowly whisking in the flour until fully absorbed. Stir constantly to avoid scorching for about 30 to 40 minutes until roux achieves a nut-brown color, then add vegetables to roux and cook until limp. Add roux and vegetables to heated chicken stock. Roux mixture and stock should be approximately the same temperature to avoid overboiling or separating. Stir in herbs and spices (except salt and pepper), mixing well, and simmer for 30 to 40 minutes. Add salt and pepper as recommended, or to taste, last. Allow gumbo to cool slightly before adding diced chicken and andouille sausage. Yields 2 gallons.

Serving Suggestions

Gumbo gathers flavor when allowed to "set" for 24 hours. Reheat slowly to avoid overcooking chicken and sausage. Serve in a bowl over ½ cup of long grain white rice or, for a special flavor sensation, brown rice. Garnish with diced scallions or minced parsley.

Entrees and Appetizers

OYSTERS FERROE

> 36 fresh, medium-sized oysters
>   in shells
> rock salt
> ¼ cup clarified butter
> ¼ tsp. garlic, minced
> 1 lb. lump crabmeat
> 1 tbs. green onions, finely
>   chopped
> ¼ cup sherry
> white pepper to taste
> salt to taste

Preheat oven to 375 degrees. Shuck the oysters, reserving the bottom shells, and drain but do not rinse them. Place oysters on the bottom shells and arrange them on a bed of rock salt in six pie pans. Cook for 10 minutes.

Meanwhile, put the clarified butter into a large skillet and heat it until it is bubbling. Add garlic, stirring to distribute evenly around pan. Add crabmeat and sauté until the crabmeat is evenly heated (3-5 minutes). Then add the green onions, sherry, salt, and pepper, and sauté the mixture for a minute more until all the ingredients are well blended.

Remove oysters from the oven. Spoon crabmeat mixture over each oyster. Top this combination with enough hollandaise sauce (see recipe below) to cover the crabmeat. Return the oysters to the oven for 2 or 3 more minutes. Serve immediately. Serves 6.

Hollandaise Sauce

> 6 eggs (room temperature)
> ½ cup fresh lemon juice
> 1 tsp. chicken base
> ¼ tsp. cayenne pepper
> 4 sticks margarine

Combine in a blender eggs, lemon juice, chicken base, and cayenne pepper at high speed for 30 seconds. Heat margarine until it starts to bubble, being careful not to brown it. With the blender on high speed, add the margarine in a slow, steady stream until all the ingredients are well blended. Transfer the sauce to the top of a double boiler and cook over low heat, whisking constantly until it is thickened. Remove from heat. (The sauce may become lumpy or separate if cooked too long or at too high a temperature.) This hollandaise is lower in cholesterol than most since it uses whole eggs instead of just yolks and margarine instead of butter.

SHRIMP PIES

> 2 qt. water
> 1 lb. gumbo shrimp
> 1 tsp. white pepper
> ¾ tsp. rosemary
> ½ cup butter or margarine
> ½ cup flour
> chopped parsley
> pastry shells

Boil shrimp in water, reserving stock. Peel shrimp and return shells to stock, simmering for one-half hour. Strain out shells, adding pepper and rosemary, and bring to a boil. Separately make a light roux by heating butter or margarine and flour. Add to stock and boil for five minutes. Add shrimp to mix until they are heated. Spoon into pre-baked pastry shells and garnish with chopped parsley. Serves 4-6.

ESCARGOTS AUX CHAMPIGNONS (SNAILS IN MUSHROOM CAPS)

> **one dozen large mushroom**
> **caps, cleaned and trimmed**
> **3 tbs. butter**
> **¼ cup white wine**
> **1 dash black pepper**
> **1 dash salt**
> **½ tsp. garlic powder**

Melt butter in a skillet, add mushrooms and seasonings, sauté briefly, add wine and cook until reduced.

Snail butter

> **3 tbs. softened butter**
> **1½ tsp. garlic, chopped**
> **1 tbs. white wine**
> **1 tsp. chopped parsley**
> **1 dash Tabasco sauce**
> **1 dozen snails**

Mix together all ingredients but snails. Rinse snails and stuff into sautéed mushroom caps, putting butter mixture beneath and on top of snail. Place in a flameproof baking dish. Broil snails in mushroom caps until butter is sizzling. Serves 2.

STUFFED FLOUNDER

12 flounder fillets
½ lb. lump crabmeat
½ lb. small shrimp, cooked &
diced
1 tbs. butter or margarine
1 tbs. flour
1 cup cream
¼ cup bread crumbs
¼ cup green onions, diced
1 dash white pepper
1 dash cayenne pepper

Heat butter or margarine, add flour, and stir, but do not darken flour. Add cream slowly and bring to a boil. Combine with all other ingredients but flounder in a bowl and refrigerate until chilled. Cut flounder lengthwise into 1"-wide strips. Fold flounder strips around a 2 oz. nugget of the stuffing and stand them upright. Bake in a 350° oven for 25 minutes. Top with velouté sauce (below). Serves 8.

Velouté Sauce

2 tbs. fish or shrimp stock
¼ cup dry white wine
¼ cup water
½ bay leaf
1 tsp. garlic, minced
¼ cup heavy cream
3 tbs. butter
1 tbs. flour

Add liquids, spices, and stock to saucepan, boil, and remove after 10 minutes. Make a light roux by heating 1 tbs. butter in a pan, stirring in flour, and heating until light brown. Add roux to mixture and whisk in remaining butter.

TROUT OR REDFISH DECATUR

2 tbs. celery, diced
¼ cup onion, diced
2 scallions, chopped
2 tbs. red pepper or pimento,
   diced
½ cup sliced mushrooms
2 large tomatoes, skinned and
   chopped
½ cup virgin olive oil
1½ tsp. Tabasco sauce
3 tbs. lemon juice
3 tbs. red wine vinegar
½ tsp. salt
2 tsp. cracked black pepper
2 jalapeño peppers, seeded and
   sliced
1 lb. shrimp, cooked and
   peeled
1 lb. lump crabmeat
6 or 8 fillets of trout or redfish

Blend all other ingredients together in a large mixing bowl before
adding shrimp and crabmeat. Refrigerate and allow to marinate
for six hours. Bake fish at 350° for 20 minutes, spoon sauce over
after baking, and broil slightly before serving. Serves 6-8.

The oyster, that noble bivalve, is as much a festive part of New Orleans culture as Mardi Gras. In the nineteenth century, gentlemen supped at their clubs upon Louisiana's bounty in season, sipping the oysters right from their shells, unadorned. Creole cookery evolving in the twentieth century has taken this feast to new heights through rich, supple sauces that are easy to prepare. Here are three New Orleans favorites that serve to dress up any occasion as hors d'oeuvres or as a main course.

Master Recipe

Secure from a reputable seafood purveyor only fresh oysters in their shells. Jarred oysters, while suitable for many purposes, are not quite as fresh and lack something in quality and consistency. Shuck in the normal manner and place the half shell in a baking pan or pyrex dish on a bed of rock salt, both to keep the shells steady and to hold additional heat against them. Top with the sauce of your choice from below and bake in a 350° oven for 20 minutes, turning on the broiler at the end to brown slightly. Plan on serving six per person for an appetizer and a dozen or more as a main course. Place in the rock salt on the half shell. Voilà!

OYSTERS ROCKEFELLER

1 clove garlic, minced
1 tbs. celery, minced
1 green onion, minced
3 tbs. white onion, minced
1 tbs. parsley, minced
2 tbs. butter
2½ tsp. Worcestershire sauce
1 bag fresh spinach
1½ tbs. anchovy paste
½ cup Herbsaint or Pernod
1¼ cups chicken stock
3 tbs. butter
3 tbs. flour

Wash spinach thoroughly and cook down by placing in a pan on low to medium heat, covering, and stirring often. Drain and set aside. Mince and combine all other vegetables and sauté in 2 tbs. butter and Worcestershire in a large skillet until soft, adding the spinach at the end. Transfer the mixture to a Cuisinart or blender, add the Herbsaint and anchovy paste, and mix for five seconds. Wipe down the sides with a spatula and mix again for five seconds. In the skillet prepare a roux with three tablespoons of butter and three of flour, browning slightly. Whisk in the chicken stock and bring to a boil, then spoon in the spinach mixture, stirring constantly until the mixture thickens and the stock is absorbed. Spoon generously over each oyster. Covers approximately 36 oysters.

OYSTERS BIENVILLE

½ lb. medium shrimp, heads on
   if possible
1 quart shrimp stock (reduced)
1 green onion, finely diced
3 tbs. parsley, finely diced
¼ tbs. garlic, finely diced
1 cup mushrooms, chopped
1 tbs. clarified butter
2 tbs. butter
2 tbs. flour
1 tbs. bread crumbs
⅛ cup Parmesan cheese
2 ounces white wine
½ tsp. salt
½ tsp. Tabasco sauce
½ tsp. white pepper

Bring three to four quarts of water to a boil, add shrimp, and reduce heat. Poach shrimp seven minutes, then remove from stock, reserving 1¼ quarts for later use. Peel and dice shrimp, returning heads and shells to stock. Cook 20 to 30 minutes over high heat, reducing liquid to one quart, and strain to remove shells. Finely dice vegetables and sauté in 1 tbs. butter until soft, adding the mushrooms last. In a large saucepan create a roux with two tablespoons of flour and two of butter, darkening slightly. Slowly whisk in reduced shrimp stock until well blended and thickened. Add cheese, spices, wine, bread crumbs, and 1 tbs. butter. Remove from heat and add vegetables and shrimp, stirring periodically until set. Spoon over oysters generously and bake per master recipe. Covers approximately 36 oysters.

OYSTERS COURT OF TWO SISTERS

1 tbs. clarified butter
2 stalks green onion, minced
2 tbs. white onion, diced
2 tbs. parsley, chopped
½ tsp. garlic, pureed
2 cups fresh oysters in their
    water
1 small can artichoke hearts
2 tsp. salt
½ bay leaf
1 tsp. thyme
3 tbs. butter
3 tbs. flour
½ cup black olives, chopped
½ tsp. Tabasco sauce

Sauté the onions, parsley, and garlic in 1 tbs. butter until soft. Separately, bring oysters and artichoke hearts to a boil with ½ bay leaf and thyme for ten minutes and drain, reserving stock. Roughly chop oysters, black olives, and artichoke hearts in a blender or Cuisinart and recombine with stock, cooking for 20 minutes. Create a light roux separately with three tablespoons of butter and three tablespoons of flour and add to mixture until thickened. Remove the sauce from heat and add salt and Tabasco. Top oysters, bake per master recipe, and enjoy. Covers approximately 36 oysters.

OYSTER PASTA

1 dozen oysters
3 tbs. onion, diced
3 tbs. bell pepper, diced
3 tsp. Toulouse seasoning (see
   below)
½ lb. mozzarella cheese, grated
½ lb. rotini pasta
1 pint whipping cream
2 tbs. butter

Poach oysters in their own liquid and set aside. Sauté onions, bell pepper, and Toulouse seasoning with 2 tbs. butter. (Toulouse seasoning is a combination of salt, white pepper, black pepper, onion powder, cayenne pepper, paprika, and thyme in equal amounts of one tablespoon each.) Whisk in whipping cream until thickened. Add cheese gradually, stirring constantly, then allow to simmer for 15 minutes. Cook pasta until al dente. Place pasta in casserole, add oysters, pour sauce over pasta and serve. Serves 6-8.

CRABMEAT ST. PETER

This dish uses many of the ingredients used in Crabmeat Rector, another favorite of our Royal Street regulars.

¼ lb. butter
2 tbs. shallots, diced
2 stalks green onion, diced
¾ cup bell pepper, diced, both
   green and red
3 tbs. parsley, chopped
1 cup mushrooms, sliced
1 lb. lump crabmeat, picked
   clean of shell
1 cup white wine
½ tsp. salt
1 tsp. black pepper
1 tsp. white pepper
1 tsp. cayenne pepper
1 tsp. basil, crushed
1 tsp. onion powder
steamed rice

Melt butter and add onions and mushrooms, sautéing until tender. Add peppers and seasonings and simmer for five minutes. Add crabmeat and sauté just until the crabmeat is hot, then add the wine and simmer until absorbed and reduced. Remove from heat and let stand momentarily. Serve over steamed rice. Serves 6-8.

TROUT WELLINGTON

The finny cousin of the noble Beef Wellington, this New Orleans classic makes maximum use of the abundance of our Gulf estuaries. Served en croûte, the poached trout is covered thoroughly with the delightful Seafood Orleans sauce and baked.

> **6 or 8 trout fillets**
> **6 or 8 sheets of pastry dough**
> **1 cup dry white wine**
> **1 egg, beaten**

Poach trout fillets in dry white wine five to seven minutes, leaving the fish still firm to the touch. Allow to cool. Place each fillet in a rectangle of puff pastry sufficient to wrap completely. Smother the fillet generously with Seafood Orleans (see below). Pinch edges of pastry together, sealing with an egg wash. Bake in 375-degree oven on greased baking sheets 20 to 25 minutes or until golden brown. Serves 6-8.

SEAFOOD ORLEANS

> **½ cup butter**
> **2 tbs. celery, diced**
> **½ cup white onion, diced**
> **⅓ cup bell pepper, diced**
> **½ cup mushrooms, sliced**
> **3 tbs. parsley, chopped**
> **1 bay leaf**
> **1 clove garlic, minced**

4 cups fish stock (made from head bones and fish trimmings in equal amounts of dry white wine and water simmered 45 minutes)
¼ cup flour
¼ cup butter
1¼ lbs. shrimp
1 qt. oysters and their juice
1 lobster, steamed and diced
3 tbs. Toulouse seasoning mix (see below)
½ cup scallions, diced
¼ cup dry white wine
1½ tsp. paprika

Sauté vegetables, bay leaf, and garlic in ½ cup of butter until translucent. Add shrimp, oysters, and lobster pieces and cook over medium heat. Add seasonings and fish stock (Toulouse seasoning is a combination of salt, white pepper, black pepper, onion powder, cayenne pepper, paprika, and thyme in equal amounts of one tablespoon each), then bring to a boil. Make a light roux of ¼ cup of butter and ¼ cup of flour and add to the seafood stock. Stir in thoroughly and add wine, lower to a simmer, and cook an additional five minutes. Remove from stove.

STUFFED CORNISH GAME HEN

6-8 hens
3 tbs. butter
⅓ cup white onion, diced
⅓ cup celery, diced
⅓ cup bell pepper, diced
2 cups cooked wild rice
½ tsp. salt
½ tsp. black pepper
1 cup andouille sausage,
   ground or chopped fine
melted butter

Sauté diced vegetables in butter and add sausage, and cooked wild rice. Blend together and stuff hens. Place stuffed and trussed boneless game hens on a baking rack over 2 cups water and brush generously with melted butter. Bake in 350° oven approximately one hour, switching to broil for the last five minutes to complete browning. Add salt and pepper before serving. Serves 6-8.

ROAST DUCK WITH CUMBERLAND SAUCE

ROAST DUCK

one duck
grapefruit sections
orange sections

Halve one Long Island duckling, prick skin thoroughly with a fork, and rub exterior with salt. Roast skin side up in roasting pan with ½ cup water in bottom for 25 to 30 minutes at 350°. Remove duck from oven. Put on a plate and surround with grapefruit and orange sections. Generously ladle on Cumberland sauce and serve immediately.

Cumberland Sauce

> **1 cup currant jelly**
> **1 cup orange juice**
> **¼ tsp. dry mustard**
> **2 dashes Tabasco sauce**
> **1 oz. dry sherry**

Combine ingredients in a saucepan, heat, and mix until thickened and smooth. Reserve warm. Makes 2 cups of sauce.

BISCUITS

> **3 cups flour, sifted**
> **1 tbs. baking powder**
> **1 tbs. sugar**
> **¼ cup margarine (softened)**
> **1½ cups buttermilk**
> **1 tsp. salt**

Combine all dry ingredients in a mixing bowl, cut in margarine and add milk, blending together by hand. Knead dough well and roll out on a floured surface to ½" thickness and cut biscuits with a cutter. Place on an ungreased cookie sheet and bake at 350° for 25 to 30 minutes until golden brown. Makes 12 or more biscuits.

GRILLADES

1 lb. veal cutlets, trimmed and
   flattened with a mallet
1 cup flour
1½ tsp. cayenne pepper
1 tbs. black pepper
1 tbs. white pepper
1 tbs. garlic salt
¼ cup cooking oil

Cut cutlets into medallions and flatten with a mallet between sheets of wax paper to avoid tearing. Mix flour and spices and dredge the cutlets in the mixture. Brown both sides in oil, about two minutes each. Place in a heavy skillet and simmer covered with gravy and vegetables (see below) about one-half hour until tender. Serves 6-8.

¼ cup bacon grease
¼ cup flour
1 qt. water
1 tsp. white pepper
1 tsp. black pepper
1 tsp. cayenne pepper
1½ tsp. salt
1 tbs. garlic paste
3 tbs. butter
1 bell pepper, julienned
3 tbs. celery, sliced
1 cup onions, diced
¾ cup mushrooms, sliced
2 tomatoes, peeled and diced

Create a roux with bacon fat and flour, heating until dark chocolate brown. Add seasonings and spoon into heated water in a large saucepan. Cook over moderate heat for one hour. Sauté pepper, celery, and onions, then add mushrooms and finally tomatoes, cooking to reduce slightly. Add to gravy and simmer for 15 minutes. Add to grillades and prepare as described above.

BARBECUED SHRIMP

One of the great traditions of New Orleans Creole cooking is its flair for creativity. Often complex, this creative urge occasionally takes a turn toward absolute simplicity. Here's one of our best New Orleans originals—barbecued shrimp. Buy plenty of napkins; this is a hands-on dish!

48 large shrimp, heads on
4 tbs. ground black pepper
½ tsp. cayenne pepper
½ lb. melted butter
1 cup water
½ lb. melted butter
(absolutely no salt)
French bread

Select 48 (approximately 2½ lbs.) 16-20 count shrimp with heads on and place in a shallow baking dish large enough to contain shrimp in a double layer. Add water and one half pound of butter. Sprinkle shrimp with black pepper and cayenne and cover with second half pound of butter. Place in a hot oven (375 to 400 degrees) and roast for ten minutes. Turn with a large spoon and roast for another ten minutes until shrimp are an even robust pink. Serve with extra loaves of French bread to mop up the delicious liquor created by the butter and roasted shrimp. Serves 4.

CRAWFISH ETOUFFÉ

The Louisiana lobster, the noble mudbug, or, more commonly, the crawfish (not crayfish) is the quintessence of bayou fare. It appears in many disguises in various versions of soups, stocks, and garnishes. Alone, as the highlight of its own dish, you can almost taste in the crawfish the shadows of the Bayou Teche.

1 cup butter or pure vegetable oil
¾ cup flour
6 cups shrimp stock
2 lbs. crawfish, peeled
4-5 stalks green onions, diced
2 small white onions, diced
½ cup celery, chopped
2 bell peppers, diced
2 tsp. thyme
1 tbs. basil, plus one tsp.
1 tsp. garlic, minced
2 tbs. salt
1 tbs. black pepper, plus one tsp.
2 tsp. cayenne pepper
2 tsp. chili powder
1 tsp. ground cloves

With butter or oil and flour, make a roux until almost a caramel color. Simultaneously create a shrimp stock by boiling shrimp shells and heads frozen previously for use in 6½ cups of slightly salted water at least ½ hour. Once roux is done, add Cajun cooking's Holy Trinity (white onion, celery, and bell pepper), sautéing in the roux until soft, then gradually sprinkle in seasonings and garlic. Add the crawfish to the roux and mix briefly before folding into a stockpot of the strained, hot shrimp stock, stirring until smooth. Simmer over low heat for ½ hour, adding diced green onions ten minutes before serving. Etouffé can be served with or without rice. Serves 6-8.

JAMBALAYA

Everyone knows the famous musical refrain that begins, "Jambalaya, crawfish pie, and filé gumbo. . . ." Jambalaya has become one of the heart and soul dishes of Cajun culture. Our version of this earthy favorite is served daily at Jazz Brunch.

> 1 lb. smoked sausage
> 2 chickens (small fryers)
> ¼ lb. butter
> 1 white onion, diced
> 1 green pepper, diced
> 4 celery stalks, diced
> 4 cups rice
> 1 large can tomatoes, crushed
> 3 tbs. tomato paste
> 2 tbs. parsley, chopped
> 1 bunch green onions
> 1 tbs. salt
> 8 cups water

Quarter and cook chicken in 8 cups of water until done. Remove and allow to cool, reserving stock. Sauté white onion, pepper, and celery in butter until clear in a large Dutch oven or stockpot. Strain chicken stock and add to vegetables. Blend in tomatoes, tomato paste, and smoked sausage. Add rice and cover, cooking about 25 minutes until done. Remove chicken meat from bone and fold into rice mixture along with parsley and green onions, and simmer over low heat another 30 minutes or so until all flavors are melded. Add salt. Spike liberally with Tabasco sauce when serving. Serves 6-8.

SHRIMP TOULOUSE

The Court of Two Sisters developed Shrimp Toulouse as a sister to Shrimp Creole. It also closely follows its cousin, Crabmeat St. Peter, utilizing many of the same ingredients and touches.

½ lb. butter
1 tbs. shallots, diced
2 green onion stalks, diced
¾ cup bell pepper, diced
¼ cup celery, minced
1 cup mushrooms, sliced
3 lbs. large shrimp, headless,
    peeled, and deveined
1 cup dry white wine
½ tsp. salt
1 tsp. black pepper
1 tsp. cayenne pepper
1 tsp. white pepper
1 tsp. thyme
1 tsp. onion powder
3 tbs. parsley, chopped
toast points or puff pastries

Sauté all vegetables but mushrooms in butter until soft, then add shrimp and mushrooms together, simmering until shrimp are bright pink. Add seasonings and then wine, reducing slightly for up to five minutes. Remove from heat and let stand two to three minutes. Serve over toast points or in a puff pastry. Serves 6-8.

SHRIMP CREOLE

Perhaps the best known of all Creole dishes, Shrimp Creole is widely prepared throughout the state of Louisiana in many forms. Ours at

The Court of Two Sisters is a citified version of the bayou favorite, guaranteed to deliver sweet, succulent shrimp flavor with just enough zest to pop you out in a mild perspiration. Fire-eaters should keep their supply of McIlhenny's Tabasco sauce handy.

¼ lb. butter (1 stick)
1 cup bell pepper, diced
1 cup onion, diced
1 cup celery, diced
1 cup shallots, diced
3 tbs. garlic, minced
2 cups crushed tomatoes,
   canned or fresh
2 tbs. tomato paste
1 bay leaf
3 lbs. medium shrimp, peeled
   and deveined, shells and
   heads reserved
4 cups shrimp stock
1 tsp. basil
1 tsp. thyme
1 tsp. salt
1 tsp. black pepper
1 tsp. cayenne pepper
1 tbs. lemon juice
steamed rice

Sauté pepper, onion, celery, and shallots until soft in a large saucepan; add garlic puree and bay leaf along with crushed tomatoes and paste, and simmer for 20 minutes. Separately prepare shrimp stock from heads and shells, boiling with 4½ cups of water. Add shrimp to vegetables and cook another 15 minutes, then add strained and reduced stock, lemon juice, and spices. Simmer another 20 minutes until reduced and thickened. Serve over steamed rice. Serves 6-8.

Grand Finales

No meal at The Court of Two Sisters is complete without dessert. At The Court they are displayed with a flourish with fresh seasonal fruit at the end of the buffet line for brunch and are available a la carte for dinner.

PECAN PIE

A Southern favorite and a Court of Two Sisters tradition. Remember to pronounce 'em puh CAHNS. Bake one for a friend and save one for your family.

> **1¾ cups dark corn syrup**
> **2¼ cups sugar**
> **6 egg whites**
> **1½ tsp. salt**
> **4 tbs. vanilla**
> **½ cup butter**
> **2 pie shells**
> **3 cups shelled pecans**

Arrange 1½ cups each of shelled pecans around the two pie shells and bake at 325 degrees for five minutes. While you're waiting, combine sugar and syrup in a mixing bowl. Cream in butter, eggs, salt, and vanilla. Mix on low speed for five minutes. Pour 2½ cups filling into each prepared pie shell and bake at 325 degrees for 40 minutes or until center is firm. Makes two 9-inch pies.

KING CAKE

A New Orleans tradition, especially as the Mardi Gras season approaches. This makes a wonderful office gift or a welcome alternative to coffee cake at breakfast.

⅓ **cup granulated sugar**
1 tsp. salt
½ **cup all-purpose shortening**
2 large eggs
1 cup milk (at room
   temperature)
1 pack active dry yeast
1 tsp. flavoring (lemon, orange,
   or vanilla)
4 cups all-purpose flour
vegetable oil
cinnamon sugar
granulated colored sugar

Cream white sugar, salt, and shortening well. Add eggs and continue creaming. Dissolve yeast in mixture of milk and flavoring and add to mixture. Add flour and mix until smooth. Knead by hand or in mixer until dough is smooth and pliable. Dough temperature out of the mixer should be 80 degrees F. Allow dough to rest for approximately 1½ hours. Roll out in an oblong piece. Paint with vegetable oil. Add heavy cinnamon sugar; fold to hold sugar in. Cut into three strips and plait (braid). Let rest until it can be stretched easily and made into a circle. Put colored sugar (proper Mardi Gras colors are purple, green and gold) on cake just before it goes into the oven. Bake at 370 degrees F. for approximately 12 to 15 minutes.

BREAD PUDDING

3 cups milk
1 24" loaf of day-old French bread cut into 1½ to 2" cubes (12 cups bread cubes)
1 one-lb. can fancy fruit cocktail, drained and cherries removed
1 29-oz. can peach halves, drained and cut into large chunks
⅔ cup raisins
¼ cup (½ stick) melted salted butter
4 large eggs
1 cup sugar
½ tsp. vanilla extract
1 tsp. cinnamon
¾ tsp. freshly ground nutmeg
¼ tsp. allspice
pinch of salt

Scald the milk in a heavy 4- to 5-quart saucepan. Remove from heat and allow to cool for about 5 minutes, then add the bread, fruit cocktail, canned peaches, raisins, and melted butter and mix thoroughly. In a separate bowl beat the eggs and add the sugar, vanilla, cinnamon, nutmeg, allspice and salt. Mix until thoroughly blended, then add to the bread mixture and blend well.

Butter a 3- to 4-quart earthenware or china casserole thoroughly on all inner surfaces (or use a baking dish about 3 to 4 inches deep). Pour the mixture into it and stir to distribute the ingredients evenly. Bake uncovered in a preheated 350-degree

oven for 1 hour and 10 minutes or until knife inserted in the center comes out clean and the top begins to brown and form a rough crust. Allow to cool to room temperature. Serve warm or chilled with Brandy sauce. Serves 8 or more.

Brandy Sauce

> 1¼ lbs. butter
> 1 lb. sugar
> 9 egg yolks
> ½ cup Half and Half
> 2½ ounces bourbon
> 4 tsp. corn starch mixed in ½
>   cup cold water

Melt butter and dissolve sugar over double boiler. Add egg yolks and whip vigorously so that egg yolks do not curdle. To this mixture add Half and Half and corn starch mixture. Let cook over double boiler for 5 minutes. Remove from heat and add whiskey.

BANANAS FOSTER

> 6 whole bananas, quartered
> ¼ lb. butter
> 3 cups brown sugar
> ¼ tsp. cinnamon
> 2 oz. banana liqueur
> 2 oz. brandy
> 6 dishes vanilla ice cream

Melt butter, brown sugar, and cinnamon in saucepan. Add bananas and banana liqueur. Let cook until thoroughly heated. Flame with brandy; serve over ice cream. Serves 6.

CRÊPES SUZETTE

1 cup flour
1 tbs. sugar
1 pinch salt
2 eggs
1¾ cup milk
2 tbs. melted butter
1 tsp. Cognac

Beat eggs and milk until blended. Combine dry ingredients and beat eggs and milk mixture gradually into them to make a smooth batter. Add melted butter and Cognac. Batter should be the consistency of heavy cream. Let mixture stand 2 hours. Brush a small, very hot skillet with butter. Pour a generous tablespoon of batter into the pan and tip the pan to coat it with a thin layer of batter. Do this quickly. When crêpe is brown on the bottom and bubbles appear on the top, turn it and brown the other side. Roll to shape.

Sauce

¼ lb. butter
3 whole oranges (halved)
3 whole lemons (halved)
3 tsp. super fine granulated
   white sugar
1 oz. Grand Marnier
1 oz. brandy
12 crêpes

Melt butter and sugar in pan. Squeeze oranges and lemons; place juice in pan to heat. Remove pan from burner, strain seeds with fork. Add Grand Marnier, tilt pan, and ignite. When flames die out, add crêpes. Cook 3 or 4 minutes and fold into quarters. Flame with brandy. Serve 2 per guest. Serves 6.